Some Poems for
Malaysian Schools

Some Poems for
Malaysian Schools

Tony Finch

With illustrations by the author

PARTRIDGE

To order additional copies of this book, contact
Toll Free 800 101 2657 (Singapore)
Toll Free 1 800 81 7340 (Malaysia)
orders.singapore@partridgepublishing.com

www.partridgepublishing.com/singapore

Contents

Introduction

Unlike Malay, English is not a phonetic language and the spelling of a word is not a certain guide to its pronunciation. We only have to look at 'rough', 'cough', 'through', 'though' and 'bough' which all look similar but are pronounced quite differently.

Again, unlike Malay, there is no safe rule for the emphasis on the syllables in a word – compare 'sentence' with 'pretence' or 'curtains' with 'obtains'.

It is hoped that the rhymes at the end of the lines will help with the former and students are recommended to look for words with the same rhyme. The metre of a line should help to achieve the correct emphasis and thus develop the flow and intonation of the language.

Limericks are the easiest to write and students are encouraged to write their own. Sonnets (three are provided at the end) present a much greater challenge!

Most of these poems also make a moral point and could be the subject of class discussions. But it is hoped that that students will find them humorous and simply enjoy reading them.

Ali, Mahmoud and the ghost

Ali and Mahmoud are friends; they live quite near each other.
Mahmoud's sister Rohizan wed Ali's elder brother.

Now Ali is a modest boy but Mahmoud often boasts
And always says how brave he is – he's not afraid of ghosts.

Well, one day Ali thought he'd put this to the test
And went to ask his elder brother what he could suggest.

They sat and drank some tea and talked until they had a plan.
To make it work they had to get some help from Rohizan.

A big balloon, some sturdy sticks – and Ali could complete
His grand design when Rohizan brought him a large white sheet.

With copper wire he tied the sticks, shaped like the letter T,
And on the top the big balloon was fixed most carefully.

So now the shape began to look more like a human figure;
When covered with the large white sheet it certainly looked bigger.

Then Ali tied around the 'neck' a lengthy piece of string.
He held up high the other end and watched the figure swing.

He quietly took his 'ghost' with him but wasn't ready yet.
He stood there outside Mahmoud's house until the sun had set.

He brought a ladder to the wall so he could quietly creep
Across the roof above the room where Mahmoud soon would sleep.

He waited till the lights went on and then went off again
And with a stick he gently tapped on Mahmoud's window pane.

So, lowering his 'ghost' he moved it slowly up and down.
The shrieks and yells from Mahmoud's room were heard across the town.

Now Ali pulled his 'ghost' up high and then hid out of sight
While Mahmoud cried "Oh, help me! Help!!" He'd really had a fright.

His mum and dad went in to ask just what was going on.
He said: "I've seen a ghost outside but now I think it's gone."

Then Ali climbed down from the roof and spoke to Rohizan.
They went together to explain the reason for the plan.

When Mahmoud heard the tale at first he wasn't very pleased
But soon he came to realize that, simply, he'd been teased.

So now he knows it isn't nice to boast that he is brave;
He's learned a useful lesson on just how he should behave.

Ali and Mahmoud go fishing

Ali and Mahmoud, we know, were seldom far apart
And they were happy – very soon the holidays would start.

Now both the boys had fishing-rods; it was their greatest wish
To sit down on the river bank and catch a giant fish.

A garden worm was used as bait and Ali cast his line;
Now Mahmoud did the same and then they waited for a sign.

It wasn't long before they saw Mahmoud's rod slightly bend.
He pulled and saw a little fish was wriggling on the end.

But bigger fish eat smaller fish! They'd use this one as bait.
So, casting out the line again, they settled down to wait.

Time passed and then the rod bent like a palm tree in a gale.
The two boys struggled hard but knew they really mustn't fail.

At last they managed to succeed and pulled the fish ashore.
And it was big! It must have weighed a kilogram or more.

Quite big enough for supper but a giant it was not
And so they'd use <u>this</u> one as bait and give it one last shot.

They fixed it to their biggest hook and cast it in the water
And wondered what would happen next. This time their wait was shorter.

A violent pull – the line ran out and suddenly fell slack.
"We've lost our fish." they moaned "And now we'll never get it back."

They reeled in the line again and to their great surprise
They vaguely saw a shape appear of quite gigantic size.

"We've done it! Look at that" they cried and both began to smile
Until the shape crawled up the bank – it was a crocodile!

They ran so fast they'd qualify for some Olympic race
And only stopped when sure the croc had given up the chase.

The moral of the story – when you've got just what you need
And try for more you lose the lot – the punishment for greed!

The sad story of Vijay

Vijay had a motor-bike.
It really was his brother's
But Vijay used it as he liked
And so did several others.

Perhaps his brother didn't mind
That everybody used it.
Perhaps he simply was too kind
And most of them abused it.

The steering was a bit too loose,
The brakes were much too floppy
And though it's not a good excuse
The servicing was sloppy.

It never should be on the road
And everybody knew it.
It went against the Highway Code
So why did Vijay do it?

He wanted to impress his friends
How fast he now could ride.
And this is where the story ends –
He hit a bus and died.

The case of Wen Li

Wen Li was a charming girl. Her hair was thick and glossy.
Her teeth were white, her eyes were bright. She wasn't rude or bossy.
Excelling on the playing field and happy to be active
She always found her friends around her - she was so attractive.

She studied hard, her grades were good, her teachers were impressed.
Out on the grass or in the class she always did her best.
She made her parents proud and was an asset to the school.
Of course, the boys made lots of noise and thought her pretty cool.

The problem started when one day she watched a fashion show.
The clothes were fine and well-designed – that's not what struck her so.
She suddenly decided that she'd be a model. That
Caused all the fuss which worried us: she thought she was too fat!

We knew this wasn't true at all – the models she had seen
Were far too thin – just bones and skin – but Wen Li was fifteen.
Her thoughts were concentrated now on how she must lose weight.
It was these thoughts which sadly brought her to a sorry state.

She ate no breakfast, then no lunch and hardly any dinner.
Day by day to our dismay she steadily grew thinner.
Her eyes were dull, she seldom smiled, her hair had lost its shine
And we, her friends, could see these trends and feared her sad decline.

TONY FINCH

Wen Li saw the problem when her grades began to drop
The diet fad was really bad but now she couldn't stop.
She had such little energy and soon became depressed.
This was a case that she must face; it had to be addressed.

She was taken to a hospital – it wasn't very nice.
It must have shocked her when the doctor gave her his advice.
"A course of psychotherapy – it is the only cure,"
The doctor said, "Just go ahead. It's what you must endure."

It took some months but finally Wen Li got well again.
Her grades improved and soon she proved she hadn't lost her brain.
And modelling? Oh, no! With this experience which rocked her?
Now we find she's changed her mind and wants to be a doctor.

TONY FINCH

The crimes of Lieng Sheng

Lieng Sheng was an only child;
He ran around, completely wild.
His parents' attitude was mild -
He soon learned to outwit them.

Their thinking was perhaps too woolly,
Actually they never fully
Realized he was a bully
Till one day he hit them.

Clearly something was amiss
And when they scolded him for this
He answered with an angry hiss
And in his fury bit them.

He told his parents to go hang
And slammed the front door with a bang
To go and join the local gang
And that is how he quit them.

They saw his list of misdeeds climb
He was suspected many times
Of shameless and unseemly crimes
But never would admit them.

Then finally police breakthroughs
Found evidence from many clues
Of several crimes he stood accused
With proof he did commit them.

So now he's got some years in jail
And found a life of crime will fail.
Such attitudes must not prevail –
And people won't permit them.

The quick reactions of Wei Ping

Wei Ping was walking down the street, his satchel on his back,
When suddenly he witnessed a most cowardly attack.
Two men were on a motor-bike – the action was well-planned.
A woman walking slowly held a small boy by the hand;

On her other arm she had a large, black leather bag.
Wei Ping saw the motor-cyclist make a quick zigzag;
Weaving through the traffic to the woman with the boy,
The passenger stretched out his arm – it was a clever ploy.

He quickly snatched the bag and pulled it sharply off her arm.
She tripped and fell but fortunately came to no great harm.
Wei Ping slipped his satchel off and started to give chase
And as the motor-cyclist passed he swung it in his face.

So sudden was the shock the riders fell down on the ground;
Immediately some passers-by began to gather round.
The woman came to take her bag and thank the gallant Wei Ping
While several people held the men to stop them from escaping.

Someone made a phone call and the police came to arrest them
And when they heard what Wei Ping did it certainly impressed them.
As everyone agreed – such quick reactions were just splendid
And for his bravery the boy was publicly commended.

Selvi's pet

Selvi had a kitten. It was extremely small.
It had a toy – its greatest joy –
A soft red woollen ball.

It chased it round the room and pushed it with its paws;
It jumped and pounced and watched it bounce
Against the walls and doors.

It was a happy kitten. It had such lovely fun.
And every day to watch it play
Delighted everyone.

Just like two woollen balls - one red, one marmalade
They rolled around without a sound
That's how the kitten played.

So Selvi called it Marmy from the colour of its coat.
She also saw below its jaw
A white patch on its throat.

When Selvi picked it up and stroked its head and chest
This ball of fur began to purr;
It loved to be caressed.

The weeks went by and then the months and soon a year had passed
The kitten grew as kittens do –
It seemed to happen fast.

20   TONY FINCH

Now Marmy went out hunting almost every other night.
Once on the mat a half-dead rat
Gave Selvi such a fright.

Though Selvi found it horrible it was a generous act.
Young Marmy brought it 'cos he thought it
Just what Selvi lacked.

And then one sunny morning there was a tragedy.
A big dog chased it and in haste it
Climbed right up a tree.

When Selvi heard it mew she saw the reason was quite plain.
It either couldn't or it wouldn't
Climb back down again.

She asked a friendly neighbour to bring a ladder round.
He climbed the tree and carefully
Brought Marmy to the ground.

To keep a pet is fun but know what it implies.
It's fair to say that every day
Can come as a surprise!

A surprise!

If you're in a hurry
For your vegetable curry
A banana leaf type restaurant will suffice
Where little piles of veggies
Are set out around the edges
With in the middle a large dolloping of rice.

The old tradition lingers:
You eat here with your fingers
Just as millions of us have always done.
They say the food tastes better
In this way but you can get a
Spoon if that's your thing – just ask for one.

Well, progress leads to change
And there's one that's really strange;
In fact I'd say that this one's pretty drastic.
The other day I saw
Something I'd never seen before –
I found that my banana leaf was plastic!

A well-deserved lesson

Wei Ping wasn't very big and didn't look too strong
But if you thought that he was weak – well, you'd be very wrong.

One day a bully came to him and said with little grace:
"Just give me all your money or I'll smack you in the face."

But Wei Ping gave a gentle smile and simply moved away.
The bully stared in great surprise then yelled: "Do what I say!"

Annoyed at Wei Ping's lack of fear he went to grab his shirt;
He'd teach this boy a lesson and make sure it really hurt.

But Wei Ping neatly moved aside – the bully grabbed at air.
Infuriated now, he lunged to snatch at Wei Ping's hair.

So Wei Ping made a well-timed move – again the bully missed.
"I'll get you now!" he screamed and raised a meaty fist.

He punched but Wei Ping dodged then took his arm and twisted round.
The bully flew up in the air and landed on the ground.

Back on his feet he saw his mates had laughed to see him fall
While Wei Ping stood there unconcerned and leaned against a wall.

The bully charged – he'd get revenge for all these clever tricks.
But Wei Ping moved again and so he slammed into the bricks.

Now stunned and bruised with broken arm, he was the injured party.
He didn't know that Wei Ping had a black belt in karate.

Ali's goldfish

Ali had a goldfish and kept it in a tank.
It only cost him fifty cents – it didn't break the bank!
He watched it swimming round and round.
It didn't make a single sound
But goldfish really aren't renowned
For singing. Let's be frank!

Round and round and up and down – it never seemed to rest.
Who knows if it was happy or excited or depressed?
It never smiled – it didn't wink
And no-one ever saw it blink
Perhaps it didn't need to think –
It wasn't overstressed.

True, it lacked intelligence. Of course it couldn't talk.
It wasn't quite the kind of pet you took out for a walk.
But although it wasn't very bright
It didn't get into a fight
Or need to be let out at night
To chase and hunt and stalk.

And Ali didn't get a fish to have a cosy chat;
He didn't want to stroke it. For that he'd get a cat.
He knew (he's not a stupid chap!)
It wouldn't jump up on his lap
To settle down and take a nap.
It was his fish – that's that!

Rosli's kite

Rosli built himself a kite
And painted it red, blue and white.
He fixed the string and pulled it tight;
He checked the knot – it looked all right.

The sky was blue, the sun was bright...
He took it for its maiden flight
And saw it climb with great delight.
It glittered in the brilliant light.

At first the wind was only slight
But then blew harder and despite
His holding on with all his might
The string broke free and Rosli's plight
Was clear to see. The kite gained height
And very soon was out of sight.

It gave his neighbour quite a fright
By landing on his house that night!

The yacht

Wei Jian's father one day bought a splendid yacht.
It's true – a sailor he most certainly was not
But when his neighbour bought a very large canoe
Of course he simply had to have one too.

Or preferably something even bigger –
A catamaran – maybe an outrigger.
But these proved rather difficult to find
And anyway did not look nearly so streamlined.

So yacht it was but as he was no sailor
He parked it in his garden on a trailer.
Magnificently placed in front for all the world
To see the polished woodwork, mast with sail unfurled

And rigging gently swinging in the breeze.
At least at first; but slowly, by degrees,
The wind grew stronger – soon became a gale
And put enormous pressure on the sail.

Now, making matters worse, it poured with rain.
This soaked the sail and added to the strain.
The trailer quickly rocked from side to side;
The yacht, now doomed, began to slide.

The sail, now much too heavy, dragged the mast
Which shuddered, quivered, trembled and at last

Snapped free and so began to fall;
It broke in two upon the garden wall.

The woodwork splintered and the canvas tore
The precious yacht was beautiful no more.
He really should have left it by the jetty –
The ropes now looked like overcooked spaghetti.

The moral: people trying to impress
Will very often end up in distress.

TONY FINCH

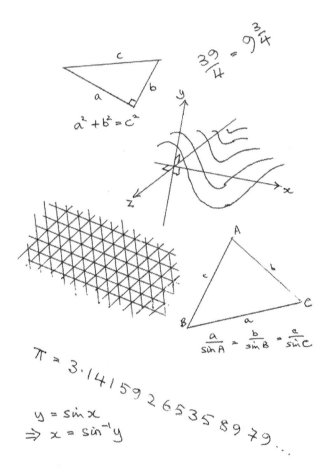

$$a^2 + b^2 = c^2$$

$$\frac{39}{4} = 9\frac{3}{4}$$

$$\frac{a}{\sin A} = \frac{b}{\sin B} = \frac{a}{\sin C}$$

$$\pi = 3.141592653589 79\ldots$$

$$y = \sin x$$
$$\Rightarrow x = \sin^{-1} y$$

Maths

I'll find a subject to amuse:
The square on the hypotenuse
Should give them such tremendous fun
More than the sum of one and one.

I must admit it's just a bore
To know that two plus two is four;
But if we want to see some action,
How about a compound fraction?

And if we really want a laugh
Let's focus on a 3D graph!
And tesselation (work on tiles)
Should have them rolling in the aisles.

Imagine, if you can, the glee
When told of trigonometry,
The rows and rows of happy faces
Counting pi to fifty places.

Just look at how their eyes will shine
While thinking of the inverse sine
And you will see them all ecstatic
Studying their mathematics.

Kumar's plan

Kumar wanted to become a star
So first of all he needed a guitar
With snazzy strap to hang around his neck
Then mikes and amplifiers (all high – tech),

Enormous speakers, keyboard, flashing lights,
Computer software using terabytes
And then a drum set – naturally the best –
He had to be much better than the rest!

Now Kumar couldn't play these instruments
And so, of course, it made good sense
To visit people at the local college
Who maybe had the necessary knowledge.

The hardest parts he'd farm out to the locals
While he, the star, would focus on the vocals.
To look the part he'd grow much longer hair
And look for some exotic clothes to wear.

He knew that he could captivate the crowd
When he got up on stage they'd soon be wowed!
He'd jump about a lot and dance and scream
He'd give a great performance – like a dream!

And sadly this is all it was – but then
Our eager, hopeful star was only ten.

The coconut

The picturesque calm of the coconut palm
As its fronds gently wave in the breeze
While you lie on the beach, a cold drink within reach,
Is an image that's certain to please.

Don't forget that the fruit is a dangerous brute
Should it happen to fall on your head!
If you lie underneath you may well get a wreath
As the chance is you'll end up quite dead.

But let's not be depressed! Note that millions are blessed
With the wealth which this fruit can provide.
You want to make curry? Well, no need to worry –
Make use of the milk that's inside.

The coconut meat is just perfect to eat
And in fact you will find it's delicious.
You really should try it – it's great for your diet
And also extremely nutritious.

If your house needs a roof then there's plenty of proof
That the fronds of the palm tree can thatch it.
And a mat on the floor or outside the front door?
Then the husk has got nothing to match it!

Now the nut, cut in two, can make cups and if you
Have the skill and can carve in good taste
Make a lovely present – so isn't it pleasant
To know that no part goes to waste!

The turtle

At night the turtle heads for land
Then slowly crawls across the sand.
She digs a hole with powerful legs
And this is where she lays her eggs.

With care she covers up the hole.
This done, she has fulfilled her rôle.
She turns around – she now is free
To make her way back to the sea.

And so she's left her little clutch
While no doubt hoping very much
That three months later they will hatch.
Unknown to her, there is a catch!

In the darkness as she leaves
Are waiting patiently some thieves
Who silently then make a dash
Towards the turtle's hidden cache.

It's cash of quite a different kind
Which callow robbers have in mind.
They steal the eggs and look for more
As several turtles came ashore.

Although the trade in eggs is banned
The thieves have all their movements planned;
They know where they can make a sale –
Attempts to catch them always fail.

Until we can enforce the law
The survival rate could be quite poor.
If no-one buys, the thieves can't sell
As everybody knows full well.

Let's do our best to stop the trade.
This simple law must be obeyed:
The theft of eggs must henceforth cease
To let the turtles live in peace.

TONY FINCH

Sibling Love
(for younger readers!)

Siti has a baby brother;
Very soon she'll have another
Or maybe she will have a sister
Said her mummy as she kissed her.

She has her books and several toys
And things which make a lot of noise
But Siti loves to help her mother
Looking after baby brother.

Although she's small and only eight
She doesn't mind her brother's weight.
She lifts him, carries him around
And never drops him on the ground.

She says quite proudly: "When I'm older
He can sit up on my shoulder!"
Perhaps she doesn't realize
That he, too, will increase in size!

She does admit she's not too happy
When she has to change his nappy
But she knows this must be done
And otherwise it's lots of fun.

The baby smiles and seldom cries
He often simply shuts his eyes
And falls asleep still fully dressed;
Now everyone can get some rest.

All is calm – no sudden screams –
I wonder if the baby dreams
Of Mum and, ready to assist her,
A loving, caring, elder sister.

Ten silly limericks

There was a young schoolgirl named Siti
Whom everyone thought was so pretty
But she dyed her hair green
In a washing machine
And she now looks a mess. What a pity!

There was a young student called Loon
Who wanted to go to the Moon.
He entered a race
And shot up into space
So he's not coming back very soon.

An extraordinary person called Shan
Had a really incredible plan.
He would eat half a ton
Of fried rice – just for fun –
And become the world's heaviest man.

A very odd fellow, Aziz,
Always wandered around on his knees.
When asked in the street,
"Why not stand on your feet?"
He would say: "I just do as I please."

I knew a young girl called Noraini
Whose hair was both wavy and shiny.
People gasped with surprise
At the size of her eyes
And her ears were so small they were tiny.

There was a young person called Lee
Who wanted to go off to sea.
So he went for a trip
On a very large ship
And he's not coming back for his tea.

An unusual fellow was Mat;
He had an extremely smart cat.
They'd sit under a tree
With a nice cup of tea
And enjoy an intelligent chat.

Two girls, Norashikin and Norma,
Were both pretty and clever. The former
Was too shy and cold
But the latter was bold
And her character therefore was warmer.

A boy on a boat trip named Ping
Just did a remarkable thing -
He lay down on the deck
With his legs round his neck
And then tied them together with string!

A young man who lived in KL
Climbed a very long ladder and fell,
Landing right on his head.
Then he got up and said:
"I really don't feel very well."

Ten even sillier limericks

There was a young boy from Johor
Who tried to go out and explore.
He didn't get far –
And this was bizarre –
'Cos he just couldn't open the door!

I knew a young schoolboy called Owen
Who was constantly to-in' and fro-in'.
The reason, I fear,
Is perfectly clear:
He didn't know where he was goin'.

Wei Ching was a very odd boy
Who always set out to annoy.
He thought it was fun
To disturb everyone
But nobody else felt much joy.

In my class there's a student called Chong
Who always gets everything wrong.
To list the mistakes
Which he constantly makes
Would take unbelievably long.

There's the story of Abdul Karim
Who had an extraordinary dream:
He began to perspire
As his hair was on fire
When he suddenly woke with a scream.

I once knew a boy called Rahim
Who came up with a wonderful scheme.
He'd get rich, so he said,
Making gold out of lead.
But, alas, it was only a dream.

A methodical girl was Azlina;
In her holiday job as a cleaner
She was given much praise
For her diligent ways -
They had never seen anyone keener.

A student of science called Kishen
Wants to practice with nuclear fission
But it's really not worth
It to blow up the Earth
So he shouldn't achieve his ambition.

There was a young man called Jalil
Who claimed he'd invented the wheel.
But they told him: "Look, mate,
You're a few years too late;
Try inventing the automobile."

A clever inventor called Din
Made a teleportation machine.
He climbed in one night
To a flash of bright light
And since then he's just never been seen.

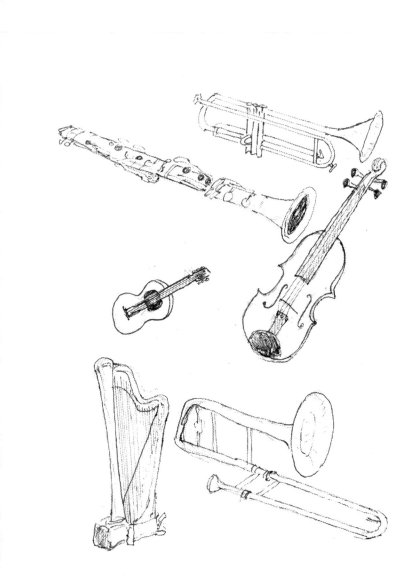

Not to scale!

Can you name these instruments?

Music

Music can make you happy
Music can make you sad
Music can even drive you mad.

Music can be soft
Music can be loud
Music can attract a massive crowd.

Music can bring memories
Music can help you forget
Music can make you do things you might regret.

Music can be popular
Music can be banned
Music can be complex or it can be bland.

Music can be heard at home
Music can be for a fancy ball
Music can need a thousand players in a concert hall.

Music can be improvised.
Music can need courses
Music can come from many different sources.

Music can be sung
Music can be played
Music can accompany a grand parade.

So what is music?

Mixed Emotions

My elder sister, my second mother,
Is getting married
And leaving home.
How I shall miss her!

Should I hate her husband
For taking her away?
Or should I love him
Because she does?

How can sadness also
Be joyful?

TONY FINCH

Sadness

To be happy
Seeing others suffer
Is sad.
To be sad
Seeing others happy
Is sadder.

The Operation

Rosli's in hospital, lying in bed
And he's bored 'cos there's nothing to do.
The patients all round him are sick or half-dead
And he wonders if he's dying, too.

A nurse hands out medicine, carefully taking
The doctor's commands to the letter.
She smiles as she asks him what progress he's making
And whether or not he feels better.

The doctor calls by, several students in tow,
And they mutter, not far from his feet.
He's got no idea what they're saying and so
He asks loudly what time he can eat.

They give him a look and the doctor comes nearer;
She prods him and asks "Does that hurt?"
The response is a scream and could hardly be clearer.
The students now look more alert.

She asks all the students to think for a while
And then guess what the young fellow's plight is.
They look at each other and one, with a smile,
Says he thinks it's a case of colitis.

"Well, you're wrong", says the doctor, "the pain's lower down
Though perhaps you are not to be blamed."
The student thinks hard and then says with a frown:
"His appendix just might be inflamed."

TONY FINCH

"Yes, it is", she agrees, "I'm afraid there's no doubt.
He must go for a quick operation;
It only takes minutes to cut the thing out."
But Rosli's afraid. Amputation?

He yells out: "I don't want you to cut me apart
And then send me back home in small pieces.
My arms and my legs and my head and my heart –
They're my own. I don't want a prosthesis!"

The doctor sits down with him, calmly explains
That there's nothing to worry about
And assures him he'll soon have no more of those pains –
There is really no reason to shout!

By the end of the week he'll be back home again
With no more than a faint little scar.
He should rest for a while and try to refrain
From running or walking too far.

So Rosli relaxes and goes for his "op".
And it's just as the doctor has told him.
Within days he is fine and is talking nonstop
But the doctor is kind and won't scold him.

He goes back to his family, feeling no pain
Though he's careful, his movements unhurried.
He is glad that it's over but doesn't complain
And admits to his friends he was worried.

But the doctor had given her word whereupon
He could see no good reason to doubt it.
And now he's relieved; his appendix is gone
And he's perfectly happy without it.

TONY FINCH

The Camping Trip

Ali went camping last week with some friends
And a couple of teachers from school.
They set up their camp where a little stream bends
As the water flows into a pool.

The nature reserve they had come to explore
Was not very far from KL
But Ali had never gone camping before
And it wasn't much like a hotel.

He had no idea how to put up the tent,
Not a clue where to knock in the pegs.
He was soon in a muddle and couldn't prevent
All the ropes getting tied round his legs.

A teacher came over to sort it all out
And quite soon had the tent up and ready.
There wasn't a pole but the wire frame no doubt
Would keep the tent rigid and steady.

The tent wasn't large but was spacious enough
To share with his good friend, Mahmoud.
Two inflatable mattresses, pillows and stuff,
Some bottles of water and food,

A few pillows, a torch and a portable fan
Spare batteries, two or three shirts -
They thought they would manage according to plan
But knew they were hardly experts!

For a while they kicked an old football about
And then went for a swim in the pool.
This was a really good place to hang out
As the water was pleasantly cool.

In the evening they lit a small fire and prepared
To cook what they could for a meal.
They'd brought veggies and meat and some rice which they shared
And set to with commendable zeal.

The boys were all hungry (they weren't on a diet!)
And ate till they'd eaten their fill.
Of course they invited their teachers to try it
And all were impressed with their skill.

They chatted a while and then went off to rest
It was hot and they stripped to their pants.
In the night Ali felt something biting his chest
And found the tent swarming with ants.

He realised quickly it wasn't a dream
And shouted to wake up his friend.
They ran out of the tent and dived into the stream –
An action I'd well recommend!

Their shouts woke the others who came out to see
What was causing this noise in the night.
Such excitement and drama! Just what could it be?
Then the teachers arrived with a light.

They soon saw the ants in a long, snaking column
Ali's tent just lay right in their path.
"We must move" said the teacher; his voice was quite solemn,
"When the two boys have finished their bath!"

They took down their tents and then carried their stuff
To the opposite side of the stream.
It wasn't much fun but then camping is rough
Or so it would certainly seem.

They were tired and wet as the stream was quite deep
But they knew what they all had to do.
They just hoped that they'd not be disturbed in their sleep
By a wandering tiger or two!

TONY FINCH

Saiful Adli's badminton

Saiful Adli is his name
And badminton's his game.
This is his sport
And on the court
He plays it to acclaim.

He takes a second to prepare;
The shuttlecock is in the air –
And then his serve
With skill and verve
And awe-inspiring flair

Sweeps down and in a flash
With unbelievable panache
The shuttlecock's
Too fast to block
So powerful is his smash.

It seems as though his legs are springs
He jumps up high and then he swings
His racket blurs
He never errs
You'd think this boy had wings!

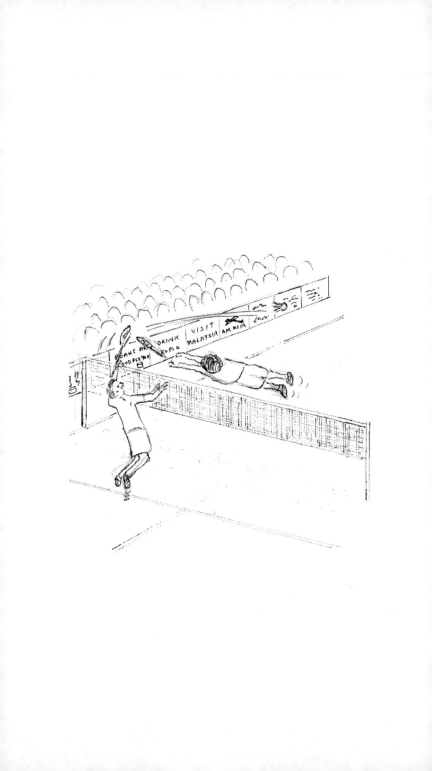

He doesn't always leap and bound
And sometimes at the net he's found -
A gentle tap –
That feathered chap
Sinks softly to the ground!

And then he'll hit it by design -
His accuracy's always fine.
He lobs it high -
Just watch it fly
And land right on the line!

His skill is certainly supreme
I'm sure he will achieve his dream –
The chance to play
And join one day
The national badminton team.

The computer addict

Tong Hai likes to watch TV
And play computer games.
He only does so when he's free –
At least, that's what he claims!

His teachers say he's fairly keen;
Exams he always passes
But too much staring at the screen
Means now he must wear glasses.

He always comes straight home from school
And takes the shortest route. A
Minute later, as a rule,
He's switched on his computer!

He doesn't take much exercise;
He never runs and that
Is why it's really no surprise -
He's getting very fat.

His diet's usually fast foods
And sweet drinks by the litre.
From this it's easy to conclude
He's not a healthy eater.

Tony Finch

And as he sees his weight increase
He starts to feel the pain.
And very soon he'll be obese;
This will affect his brain.

His neighbours hardly know him;
He doesn't have a friend.
So someone needs to show him
Just how sadly this could end.

His attitude's too laid-back
And he should be more athletic
Or else he'll have a heart attack
Or end up diabetic.

This future's not attractive
As Tong Hai just might find.
Your body must be active
To maintain a healthy mind!

TONY FINCH

The dream

When spiders sing and tigers talk
And kittens take you for a walk
When lizards laugh and seagulls sigh
And puppies want to make you cry

When mynahs moan and fruit flies frown
And monkeys hold you upside-down
When goldfish grin and sparrows scream –
You know you're living in a dream.

Then, half awake, the memories fade –
The real world is newly made.

A risky game

Mohan likes to climb a tree
And stand up on a branch.
He loves to shout and jump about;
His efforts make the whole tree shake!
Then fall in showers to the ground
To cover it almost all around
The yellow leaves, soon breaking free –
A minor avalanche!

Once in a park he stopped to stare
At one of nature's giants.
Now this was one where he'd have fun!
He climbed up high towards the sky
But went too far out on a limb
And this was dangerous for him.
Perhaps he wasn't quite aware
Of fundamental science.

His extra weight and longer distance
From the trunk was why
The branch gave way to his dismay
And with a crack behind his back
Began to fall. But he was plucky;
Grabbing branches, he was lucky
As they offered some resistance
So he didn't die!

Whose fault was it?

Danial was just fifteen; he was an only child.
He hadn't much self-discipline and usually ran wild.
His father was a businessman and seldom stayed at home.
He went on trips to Washington, to London, Prague and Rome.

His mother had her social friends. Her one and only passion
Was buying clothes and hats and shoes – all in the latest fashion.
Their idea of parenting was very odd – in essence
Because they rarely saw their son they simply gave him presents.

Computer games, a new hi-fi, a TV and much more –
Electronic gadgets filled his room and covered half the floor.
With two maids there to wait on him he had no daily chores;
He mostly stayed inside his room and rarely went outdoors.

Such irresponsibility should never be excused;
His parents spoiled him terribly and nothing was refused.
He just assumed that anything he wanted he could own.
This led to strange behaviour as experience has shown.

Of course he had to go to school; his driver took him there.
In class he had to do some work but thought this wasn't fair.
He'd never need to earn a living. Study? What a bore!
Pass exams and learn a skill? No way! Whatever for?

But then at school he saw this girl and found her most attractive.
His hormones, dormant all these years, now suddenly were active.
He had no social skills and no idea of courtesy
So simply said to her "I want you. Come along with me."

TONY FINCH

The girl, not used to this approach, just gave a nervous giggle.
He grabbed her by the arm and pulled so she began to wriggle.
At this he lost his temper and in anger slapped her face.
"Don't waste my time! Just come with me – I know a quiet place."

The girl in shock and fear cried out "Oh, someone please help me!"
Some passers-by ran up to them and quickly set her free.
An arm around his neck, a kick, and he was on the ground.
His frenzied struggles were in vain as Danial soon found.

A woman made a phone call and two policemen came.
They listened to the witnesses and soon saw whom to blame.
A man had filmed the whole attack and this, with his report,
Was taken by the officers and later used in court.

The boy was pushed into a car and thrown into a cell.
The next few weeks and months would be for him a living hell.
His parents shrugged their shoulders when they learned what he
had done.
They couldn't understand it – what had happened to their son?

It really was embarrassing to see it on the news.
His father flew to Washington. His mother bought some shoes.

Metamorphosis

I am a vegetarian and this I've always been
And I'd eat almost anything so long as it was green.
The colour of my skin was just the same – I can't deny it;
Perhaps it was the chlorophyll – so much was in my diet.

I mostly lived on lettuce leaves and simply ate and ate.
I didn't take much exercise and soon I put on weight.
I slowly crawled from leaf to leaf but life was such a bore!
Nothing ever changed – I couldn't take it any more.

And then one day I went to sleep and slept quite splendidly.
I woke to find myself bound up and struggled to get free.
And then I saw! I'd changed! No longer was I fat;
I now had wings and fewer legs. Can you imagine that!

No longer green but colourful – my wings were red and blue.
I soon took to the air – I was so proud and happy, too.
So now you can admire me when you see me flutter by.
I was a caterpillar but I'm now a butterfly!!!

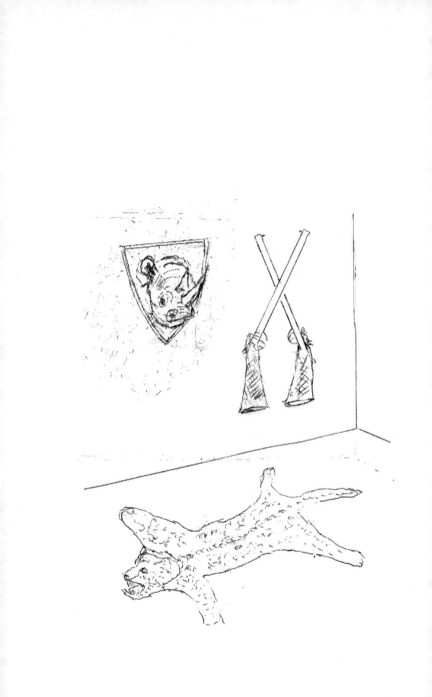

What are we doing about this?

Have you ever seen a leopard, hiding quietly and unseen?
His hearing is remarkable, his eyesight too is keen.
And when he sees his prey he bounds and runs so fast that he'll
Quickly overtake and leap so that will be his meal.
But sadly for this animal his pelt can fetch a price;
It's sold for making coats and rugs which isn't very nice.

And then there's the rhinoceros, a horn upon his nose.
He lives off plants and bushes – almost anything that grows.
His hide is armour-plated; he can weigh almost a ton
So don't approach too closely because when angry he can run!
But sadly for this animal his horn can fetch a price;
It's used for making medicines which isn't very nice.

In Africa the elephant has tusks and floppy ears,
A trunk that's long and flexible and – not as it appears –
Is actually quite sensitive – a hand and nose combined.
His sense of smell is excellent – it's really well designed!
But sadly for this animal his tusks can fetch a price
For making pretty ornaments which isn't very nice.

The tiger's very famous and you know it by its stripes
But actually we know of more than half a dozen types.
The Bengal and Malayan and Siberian are three;
Now try and find the others which may still be running free!
Though sadly, like the leopard, their pelts can fetch a price
And their habitats are threatened which isn't very nice.

There are many other animals which I could also name:
The chimpanzee and pangolin .... It really is a shame
That all these splendid creatures are so very clearly linked -
They're all endangered species and could soon become extinct.

Art in geometry
(with apologies to Longfellow)

From his satchel Hiawatha
Took his box of pens and pencils,
Took his ruler and protractor,
Took his set-square and eraser,
Took his compasses and ruler,
Took a sheet of pure white paper
And the clever little gadget
Used for sharpening his pencil
Which he did with great attention
Till the point was like a needle
And he put them on the table,
Set them out in order neatly
Ready for his great construction –
This would be a masterpiece of
Geometrical precision.

First he drew a perfect circle
Large enough to almost cover
Half the sheet of pure white paper.
Then he drew another like it,
Wholly and exactly like it;
This was drawn above the first one
So the two were overlapping,
Making sure the total distance
From one circle to the other
Was exactly thrice the distance
From one centre to the other.

Now he drew the common tangents
Of the wholly perfect circles
Accurately with his ruler.
And he picked up his eraser,
Rubbing out the lines inside the
Figure which he'd now created
To obtain a kind of oval
Like the field where players liked to
Demonstrate their skills at cricket.

Then he drew two little circles,
Drew them not too close together
With their centres in the middle
Of the oval he'd constructed
With the line which joined these centres
Normal to the common tangents.
On each tangent on the outside
Now he drew two semicircles.

Just below the little circles
Came a small three-sided figure,
All three sides were drawn quite equal -
Equilateral we call it –
With one vertex pointing upwards
Right between the little circles.

Then some little arcs were needed:
Under the three-sided figure
Like the letter U he drew one
And above each little circle
Like the letter U inverted
Drew one very slightly smaller.

TONY FINCH

Now his masterpiece was finished
And in bold italic letters
Underneath his great construction
Carefully he wrote as follows:
"Here's my Mathematics teacher."

Can you follow the directions?
See if you can draw the figure!

Common tangent = a line touching two circles
Normal = perpendicular

Things you shouldn't do

There are many things you shouldn't do: don't kill, use violence,
or steal!
If someone did these things to you, imagine how you'd feel!
There is an ancient saying which these days is just as true:
Do to other people as you'd have them do to you.

....

Some unwise things which people do are often self-inflicted,
Forgetting that the consequences can be well predicted.
Taking drugs is one case when they soon become addicted
Then they're caught and very soon they find themselves convicted –
For many years their movements are by bars and walls restricted!

But when they start they think it's great and so they try again;
And then they're on to heroin and smoking crack cocaine.
It isn't long before the pleasure turns to wracking pain.
Dependence on the drug can soon be driving them insane
As chemical reactions ruthlessly destroy their brain.

Smoking cigarettes is also certainly unwise.
Beware! A company which likes to advertise
Tobacco will say anything but never emphasise
The danger to the lungs – it is something it denies -
But it wants to make a profit so this comes as no surprise.

A final word of wisdom – be careful what you eat
And drink because this fizzy stuff is often far too sweet.
There's too much sugar in it – from the cane or from the beet;
This affects the insulin your pancreas secretes
So diabetes gets you if your body you mistreat.

Help and you will be helped

Amir was walking down the street
And saw a woman trip and fall.
He helped her to get on her feet
Then took her to the nearest stall.

She'd had a shock; she's bruised her arm
And slightly cut her hand and knee.
"Well, this won't do you any harm"
He said, and brought some hot strong tea.

She phoned a friend who brought her car
To take her home. The woman smiled;
"Thank you", she said, "You really are
A very kind and helpful child."

But then one day, quite unaware,
He dropped his wallet on the ground.
A woman's voice called out: "Hey, there,
Just take a look at what I've found!"

It was the woman he had helped;
She held his wallet in her hand.
"But that's amazing" Amir yelped,
"My thanks! It's hard to understand!"

"A strange coincidence", he thought
And that is what he told his mother.
"No," she said, "it's what we're taught –
That one good turn deserves another."

The Ring

Ali really loves to dive –
He says it makes him feel alive.
He'd go with friends out in a boat
And for a while he'd laze and float.
He'd then put on his scuba gear;
The tranquil water was so clear -
Now he could see the world below
And watch the fishes come and go.

But then one day as down he swam,
Between an oyster and a clam
He saw a most surprising thing –
He saw a pretty, shining ring.

He picked it up and quickly rose
To show it to his friends whose "Ohs
And Ahs" as they admired
The pretty ring which he'd acquired
Convinced him that this wondrous treasure
Meant for him a life of leisure.

The flashing stone must surely be
A diamond found beneath the sea.
The gold would also fetch a lot –
Was this an awesome find or not!!
He'd buy a car, a brand new phone –

He wouldn't need to take a loan.
His wildest dreams could now come true
But first was something he must do.

He took it to the town next day
And asked a jeweller what he'd pay.
Who looked and then said "No offence
But it's not even worth ten cents.
The shiny metal's only brass
The flashing stone – well, it's just glass."

We should remember what we're told:
That all that glitters is not gold.

Tony Finch

A lack of motivation

Maidin is a lazy boy; he doesn't want to learn.
His parents try to do their best – he is their great concern.
He often doesn't go to school and hangs around the malls
To meet up with like-minded friends and lounge against the walls.

And even when he goes to school he doesn't pay attention;
His teachers give him extra work and put him in detention.
His classmates try to help him but they give up in despair,
Eventually discovering he simply doesn't care.

His lack of motivation will assuredly condemn
Him as a certain failure when he takes his SPM.
There is a famous saying which applies to him, I think:
You can lead a horse to water but you cannot make it drink.

The road to success

Shahirah got up before six in the morning
And took out her books for the day.
She looked at each subject and read the next chapter
To see what the teacher would say.

When a sale was announced in the town where she lived
She made sure she was first on the scene.
Whatever she did she would plan in advance
To succeed; this became her routine.

She was always the first to find bargains on e-bay
And bought several gifts for her friends.
She studied the markets, she read about futures
And learned how to follow the trends.

She took a degree in accounting and finance;
Her attitude goes to confirm
That success means you must be proactive. Remember:
The early bird catches the worm!

Be careful!!

There are always some confidence tricksters around
And gullible people can often be found.
They buy shares in a gold mine which doesn't exist –
A wonderful option which mustn't be missed!

Or they fall for a sweet-talking con artist's pitch
That a magical stone will ensure they'll be rich.
These criminals' methods are terribly clever
And poor peoples' money is soon gone forever.

So if somebody claims you can make lots of money
By giving them cash it may not be so funny.
I strongly advise you – just give them the push
'Cos a bird in the hand is worth two in the bush.

Choose your friends wisely!

It's good to have friends but make sure they don't use you.
At the start they may try – and succeed – to amuse you
But then could play tricks and begin to confuse you
And get you to do things so others accuse you.

So be perfectly clear
That they're really sincere.
You'll get some odd looks
If your friends are known crooks
And people will say
That you've been led astray –
Thinking birds of a feather
Will all flock together.

Sivan's parrot

Sivan has a parrot and he calls the bird Enkili.
It happily eats fruit and nuts but doesn't much like chilli.
Its wings are multicoloured and it has a long curved beak.
Sivan often strokes it and has taught it how to speak.

It's very tame and flies around quite freely every day;
It's pleased to be with Sivan and will never fly away.
It sometimes sits on Sivan's head and gently pulls his hair;
Both in the house and garden it goes with him everywhere.

And when it's time for bed he chains it lightly to a bar.
Before it sleeps it practises its English repertoire!
But then one night someone forgot – the window wasn't shut
And Enkili contentedly was chewing on a nut

When suddenly it heard a noise and loudly flapped its wings:
A burglar'd entered secretly to try to steal some things.
"What is your name?" Enkili squawked and then "How do you do?"
The burglar, startled and in shock, knew what he had to do!

It was too dark inside the room – he could not clearly see
And so decided that the best thing he could do was flee.
Everything was quiet again as soon as he had left
And Sivan never knew that his Enkili'd foiled a theft!!

Sonnet No. 1
– Consequences

In recent years the progress we have made
In transport, education, public health
Must recognize the role which has been played
By industry which fuels our growing wealth.
We all enjoy these benefits although
The cars and motorcycles which we own
And use of electricity all show
How much the need for energy has grown.
But now that greenhouse gases are released
And CO_2 and methane fill the air
The threat of global warming has increased.
The consequences may be hard to bear;
We now discover to our tragic cost
That all we have could sadly soon be lost.

Sonnet No. 2
— Stop this pollution!

Plastic bags are strewn beside the roads;
They lie discarded, ugly, on the beach
And in the rivers where some fool unloads
His rubbish. Is this what our parents teach?
Does civic conscience have no meaning now?
I hope these are the actions of the few
And most of you will readily allow
That surely they don't beautify the scene.
Are paper bags so difficult to use? –
Or cotton or some other cloth that's made?
There are so many we could choose
Which, unlike plastic, can quite easily degrade.
Because unless we change we could be faced
With drowning in a sea of plastic waste.

Sonnet No. 3
— Astrology is not a science.

The fading shades of day expose the night
And, far above, the brilliant points appear.
They give no heat and only meagre light
At such enormous distances from here.
For long before we humans came to be
The stars' dispassionate regard, unchanged,
Has cast on Earth their nightly glow. Yet we
Imagine that they somehow have arranged,
Through pictures in the sky we seem to find,
Our fate – and their advice we then believe,
With credulous and superstitious mind,
From columns in the papers. How naïve
To think they guide humanity's affairs!
Our daily lives are no concern of theirs.

Printed in the United States
By Bookmasters